Mama Teach Me!

Written by **Wendy Belice**

Illustrated by **Amara Huzaifah**

Copyright © 2020 Wendy Belice

All rights reserved. No part of this publication may be reproduced, distributed or transmitted in any form or by any means, without prior written permission.

ISBN: 978-0-578-74711-8

Printed in the USA

Dedicated to my son Eddy. You make life more beautiful!

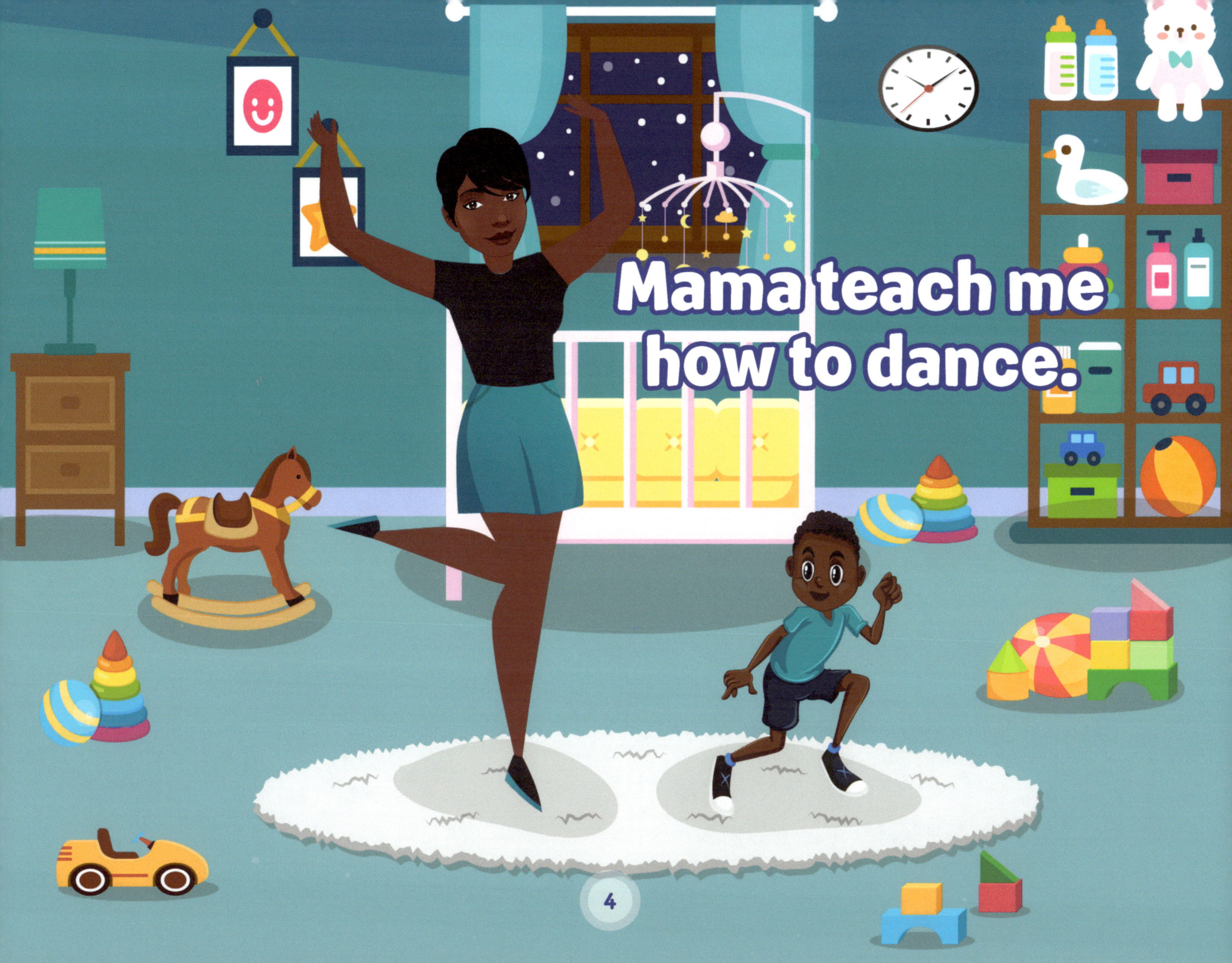

www.ingramcontent.com/pod-product-compliance
Lightning Source LLC
Chambersburg PA
CBHW041324290426

44108CB00004B/122